To Jenny

Lunch on a
Green Ledge

With all best wishes,

Stella Davis

Stella Davis

Stairwell Books //

Published by Stairwell Books
161 Lowther Street
York, YO31 7LZ

www.stairwellbooks.co.uk
@stairwellbooks

ISBN: 978-1-913432-60-7
Cover Art: Dawn Treacher
p10

Also by Stella Davis

Last Boat to Avalon
Watershot
St Swithuns's Day

To Arthur Howard: "He"

Table of Contents

Last Heron

As the last heron goes, rooks
fall from the sky like old black rags
to carpet the new-laid field.
Six days
now, six days and nights
without rain falling.

We feel reprieved, for all the sullage
washing through thoroughfares,
grey-brown, dingy, dismaying.

Journeys are slow, and everything
boots clothes wheels mudguards
silts up, as we edge forward.
                              Strange
how little it matters, this besmirching,
which once would have made us think twice.

It is enough that we can go forward,
enough to watch the land-birds
wheel down onto clear earth, peck
where crops once grew, may grow
again. As now seems possible.
We wake, amazed,
from a long dream of drowning. ⁄⁄

From Chantry

The lane from the Chantry
slathers up for the season,
closes its wintry way
to all but the booted,
the sure-footed, those
with a reason for going
as the crow flies.

The crow does not fly, but hangs
from the gamekeeper's gibbet,
sleeper's peripheral nightmare
of beaks and claws.
Under the mud
runs the living briar,
flourishing of thorn.

At the little door, a cast
of dwindled sorrows.
Under the floor,
two dozen lasts. Once wide,
the way from the Chantry holds
its narrow secret,
buried forlorn.

Darkness, cloud-night, inky
from hall to cottage. The old woman
turns confidential: "My grandfather
had an affair with Miss Young.
There was a child."
Stares at me, with my cousin's
bright black eyes. //

Down West

Coming up Boundhay
in the stark of December
the man from the Odcombe eyesore says
TOO COLD TO SNOW, in capitals
as emphatic as the notice
on the gate he vaults: TRESPASSERS
will be SHOT.
Down West
we like a bit of fun
amongst ourselves.
                    A ferret
hisses a greeting
from the verge of Camp Road,
ignoring the flight of redstarts,
and the boy racers
defying death.

Two enormous herons
stalk the drowned field. *Good skating
if that lot should freeze.*

As I turn down Gooseacre
the first flakes fall. ⁂

Boy

Going out again under all that blossom
armoured only in green, he catches
the summer's glancing eye.
It is full of pity. Those amiable gossips,
the birds, have rumbled him: his going
lacks heel-to-toe conviction, leaves
something unfinished, a *tabula rasa*
for all the graffiti of love.

Wait all day in the summerhouse
and you'll not see such a deal
of crafty nature's: such pride
in ignoring the iron catch,
clearing the gate, and going
out again, under all that blossom. ⁄⁄

Ted's Place

That path by Ted's place,
it's up to the Planning. Always did want
negotiation, in summer droughts
(small rocks sharp as cleavers)
as much as in seasons of mud,
where half-way down the spring breaks,
trough turns quagmire,
the badger-runs slippery as silk.

A song thrush has its anvil
on a jut of Ham stone.

Won't pave it, will they? Good enough
for Ted, going over
to Coker, those 80-odd years
from boyhood shortcut (*Moved there
when I were eleven, no, going on twelve -
almost a working lad),*
to old man's impossible journey, even
propped on tough oak crutches.
                              The new house
takes shape, covers
that much of the garden,
part of the orchard too;
looks like it's mostly windows: for the View.

They'll be laying pipes, soon, where badgers
have nudged great primrose-drifts, white violets,
periwinkles, all uprooted to make way
for the Electric, for Mains water, stuff
Ted never bothered with:
the well, the oil lamp, useless survivors
since that hard winter exhausted
the firewood, then the man. ⁄⁄

Rogue

5.a.m., and the safe house goes rogue,
the soft stuff suddenly unguarded.

Something hungry
hesitates on the stairs

listens for the guard's
retreating sigh.

Far away in the hart's forest, tongues
keep secrets, green and curling. ⁂

First Warmth and Infusoria

Leaf-steam gets welcoming
in January when the dead mass
that was honeysuckle
secretly greens, and too-early
foliate celandine tries
a heart-wrought thing
out of body, surfacing
from soil's claggy life. Warm
in the unforked, change is becoming.

Boots on and disgraceful jacket,
I stump down to the heap,
stand, listening:
spade up, fill rainwater
buckets with mulchy diggings,
mix, pause, each breath
hard and heavy, rasping
triumphant, sunlit.
Vessels stand brimming.

Slow animacula are swimming
tentaculate, in a dream of decay.
Singular, ciliated, they drift
gracefully at play
in their world of rot, flourish
here in the composting;
lovely guarantors of the end of being,
they lap at the start
of yet another Spring. ⁄⁄

Over to Camelot

It's a place to look, as buzzards do, a realm
of possible things not manifest elsewhere:
old stories, alternative endings,
lost aunts, a teem of Irish cousins,
bi-coloured eyes, a different jest.

Something of a climb. Deliberating,
allowance is made for a certain amount of magic,
for pretty dreams gone haywire,
for orphans un-orphaned,
and a heroine more than flawed,
though not necessarily tragic.

The wind's as quick as a ferret inside loose clothing,
a particular discomfort, commensurate
with what perhaps is only
a bald green stretch,
a feral hunting-ground:
this height of unanswered yearning. ⁄⁄

Folly

Moss loves it, and a ragged squirrel
thinks it worth chattering for; but there's no doubt
humans have given this place the go-by:
Wessex is full of follies, not the least
a wish to outreach the sky.

Accretions of age have stumbled with me
over the broken doorstep: dusts and crumbs
of deserted seasons, owl pellets and mousebones,
the reddish weathering silt of little bricks.
But the stairs are not much worn: they rise
in a confident spiral, clean-edged, sharp,
and climbing one would say they're scarcely trodden,
scarcely visited, then, or now.

Yet we know that she was here, in a dusky
rustle of skirts, and there he was, and here
they sat, hands joined, on the broad stone ledge
protected by leaded crimson glass, though now
a thrusting alder branch fragments it,
strews the pieces on the turret's floor
like pools of jagged blood. Outside
the view falls back and back, across
the harvest fields and the plunge to the sea.

All summer through two ring-doves roosted here,
and turning for a final look I catch
their upward flutter, an escape of souls.
Just as well: the bulldozer is coming;
it will soon be finished, and even I, long gone. ⁄⁄

Beached

The shore-line is full of bones, little white bones
and beached bleached branches stripped to their clean last,
fleshless and sapless among the stones,
skeletal recollections from the vast
offertory of the sea. The bird
that called so raucously at daybreak, the unfurled
leaves splayed out across the skyline of many springs,
falls back now upon the bare bones of things.

Fleshed still, vivid still, encumbered,
I sift them out, from a muddled world
of claws and tarry strings. ⌀

Lunch on a green ledge

Lunch on a green ledge
bikes sculpted to a standstill
Red Admirals on the hawkbit
Toller Fratrum a blur across the valley
of the hidden Hooke. All day
long lanes and heights and hamlets:
Dorset *profonde.*
                                        It's not
for everyone, this joyous misreading
of contour lines, brake-clenching plunges,
the punishment of knees, and pitying
of poor souls trapped in passing cars,

But on unspotted Michaelmas
it fits us like a skin,
like the turf skin, that stretches
hill to folding hill, enfolding
us to its heart, where every spin
of the wheel delivers up
a place of perfect homing.
                                        You and I
lunching on a green ledge,
stealing a march on heaven. ⁄⁄

Lost

Back then, and with deliberation
we took a wrong turn. It seemed
so daring, and like excited children
randomly empowered,
we could not resist. Further and further
we made our way, and learned
the distorted footfall
fit to carry us forward.

A few turned round to fret
by some of the waysides,
broke out, pleaded, pointed elsewhere.
We soon made it understood
that only cowards and madmen
shouted, Go back.

It seemed so laudable.
Each new accomplishment
compounded the labyrinth.
We chose our circumstance, until
circumstance chose us,
made us the culprits.

"What shouldn't have happened, did."

We try to imagine
how to un-happen this, find
it was always too late,
cursed as we are
with enormous brains
we shall never live up to,
and guilty, opposable thumbs. ⁄⁄

1967

Just once we slept in a hayloft, cushioned among sweet dry
                                                        scent
of last year's harvest, beasts moving quietly
in the barn beneath us, warm-breathed
among the small clang of their bells.

And in the morning, bread, sausage, milk,
kindliness, with this instruction:
St Gallen. Bibliothek.

Where in due course we wandered felt-slippered on the
                                                    famous floor,
unknowing, awed, while ancient codices
called out to us across eleven centuries, not quite in vain.

                                *

In Vienna we sat at on small chairs in an old apartment
                                                        block,
while Pauli, courteous, worldly, plump, beringed,
dispensed Monsoon Flush Darjeeling
in eggshell porcelain.

Took us out to look at the Schonbrunn: impressive, but
                                                    closed.
In the glassy shops, cakes too expensive to buy.
Time to head east.

                                *

And then there was the Gulhane Hotel
where we slept on the roof for five lira, some of us
with little mirrors sewn into our clothes.

Nothing now reminds me how
we reached the roof, what shifty staircases
in those hazy days.

Dozens of us, equally adrift, taking our time
in the city of three names,
unpreoccupied by history.

Now that I have seen the world shrink down around me,
I wonder at that girl who smoked hashish
from a delicate filigree pipe,

and days and miles later, stared
through a moving window
as someone (not the driver) said:
Look! Mount Ararat. ⁄⁄

A House by the Sea

Framed, borrowed, portrayed, present,
cloudy seascapes haunt the house,
drift in the interior with shells and starfish,
fossils, seaglass, stones,
blue-white-blue-grey from hallway to kitchen, and all
the spilling rooms between. Pale in the morning
their palette flows out to the terrace,
and breakfast in a bowl.

The sun will blare today, towards noon,
unanswerable. The ceiling fans will whirr,
all games that are not water-games
will falter and fail,
and ice will clink in the glass.

*

The little one whose eyes pool so watchfully
stares his food out of countenance, and will not eat,
but runs on the seashore gallant as a wave,
free as the air he lives on;
sandlark from toe to golden head, he plays
everlastingly in the sunny days, he swims
with an abandonment of joy
in the smooth-running tide.

Beyond are those who meander across the water
upright on little rafts, paddling tall and singly
in the glistening morning.
Wading out through the shallows, swimmers will greet
them,
but for the children these are not important,
being undefined besides those sanderlings
that run like wound-up toys
in the fish-flickered flow.

Enter the mer folk, far out, muscular,
back to the sea, as always
striving in clear and glassy reaches,
sweeping through the swell,
strong-arming towards a darker green,
plunging ever outward against
unknowing tomorrow.
Seawater streams from their triumphant faces.

*

At the river's mouth, a solemn child
in a quiet pool explains his bucket's cargo:
"I keep them a little while, then let them go."
Tiddlers, glinting slivers among frondy weed:
their benign captor smiles and smiles.
Tiny crabs scamper round brown toes.

Down the stream a toy boat rushes the rapids, stalls
on a makeshift dam, careers
towards a sea that is warm in its shallows,
soft to the touch. Red seaweed
left by the ebb has lost its feathery beauty,
banks in briny heaps where the clockwork birds run.
Its redolence drifts up
to the houses by the sea.

*

Tea in the afternoon:
plates and cups clean-gleaming, still
ringed with blue lines:
such durable patterning
that gives us a hold on times
other than our own,
becomes a currency, proffered
and accepted, recognised as much
as the slicing of a fruitcake, the pouring of tea.

Under the wide parasol, at a weathered table,
saltily is enacted this gentle consonance,

this sigh of contentment, just for now, and no matter
that elsewhere and otherwise
the world lies unredeemed.

*

Later, and later still, the night
slips in half-noticed,
the beaches almost empty, the windows lamplit.
Indoors the children are lulled to sandy sleep
with songs of dancing water.
Starlit, there still are bathers
moving and moving
towards the great third wave.

The moon rises over the cliff's shoulder.
The enchantment does not falter.
The sea is more than the sum of all our dreams. ⁄⁄

At 4 a.m.

That night the stars were in a conspiracy
huddling in the empyrean, muttering moonshine.

Dead as may be, they clustered and murmured and greeted,
like spies whose agenda intends a downfall.

Down there, the sea was dragged halfway up banks of shingle,
intent on salting the flatlands.

Ours to contend with, those faulty tides,
that cold dead light. It made us drift so.

Our anxious feet stumbled ankle-deep among stones
piling painfully between dips and hillocks.

They muttered about us, the stars in their multitude:
they had our number. Singly, and in showers,

they glissaded across darkness, marking the moment
our heads were to be turned, and the false step taken. ⁄⁄

Fruit Moon

Such a harvest,
under what light. By day
a southern sun
piercing intrusive
through grimy city skies,

At night, the fruit moon:
brightness so clear
even here, gazing
past high-rise,
a glimpse among towers.

Under such lights,
and as surely shining,
safe in her turret
our lovely daughter
with her little son.

Women bearing fruit
no other miracle
sustains existence

Blaze on, moon,
never outclassed, but oh
near-rivalled here:
the mother bends her head
to the tiny child.

Such fruit,
such harvests. ⁄⁄

He

Born a little too soon, you had
an elfish quality,
a touch of changeling. Enormous-eyed,
you seemed so unastonished,

while we, the old folk,
gaped at you in wonder.

Time, generous as your mother, magicked you,
plumped you up, scaled down
that eldritch glimpse, until
it disappeared.
                    These few months on,
a smiling someone, joyful-cheeked,
drawn by bright lights and green leaves waving,
entranced by music or the scrunch of paper,
you're sumptuously human.

Only, within the photo-frame
lingers your far-off early self:
patient, he seems,
and full of ancient knowledge. ⫽

Cathedral Tour

The sacred is an idea
finding its reality in stone.
Cloistered, we look at maps
and guides, while under the yew tree
stand the young, whose movements
are for once slow and careful.
                          The sacred
is perhaps their idea also,
differently realised.

The building in its stony self
invites us. An unfamiliar voice.
We have no idea how to answer,
or, having an idea,
are quickly confounded.
Our answers are anyway half-hearted:
the sacerdotal
is not as we expected.

The hot May sunshine, the drought-shine,
makes this old stone quiver
in the slow eye of curiosity.

The tour lasts an hour.

The clock, the famous clock,
captures the faithless
for a speedy prayer.

We do not know the history
of the tapestry in the choir.

The sacred is a reality
finding an idea in stone.

Now visit the Bishop's Palace, see
the finest mediaeval lavatory
in the South West. //

The Door into the Rose Garden

In Persia (as we called it), in the days before,
Rosi (as we called her) drove us north to Ramsar,
to where the Caspian was more than just a rumour,
and took us to her garden. Something (perhaps
the water melons that grew in dingy ditches)
had made us ill, and weak with heat and sickness
(so innocent, so armed by innocence),
we let her take us from Tehran, to where
the roads ran out, from where the desert
(it was August) whitened round us.

In the sun-bleached city, one long wall
was punctuated by a single door,
and Rosi had the key.

"Roses," said Rosi, "began here. Began here, in Persia."
Proudly, sweetly, she led us among beds
of rosa mundi, and her smile pressed petals
into an attar, all-pervasive scent,
the richness of the first rose of the world.

A fountain played. The gardener brought pale plums.
The air was full of petals, full of bees.
"I love my garden." Rosi's nails (all twenty)
were pure vermilion, her dark head cropped chic,
her garden Persian, her dress from Paris brief
and silky-bright: a woman of her time, her place
a rose garden, beside the Caspian Sea.

And then, oh then, we kissed her cheek,
and took our leave, and made our way
westwards to Tabriz and the border, on
and on till Europe pulled us back, away
from what we did not know was coming danger.

She fled, of course, when the time came. The door
she would not open any more concealed
a garden gone to rack, the roses lost,
their ancient heady presence crowded out
by higher stenches, their Persian name
denied in Arabic. But after all these years
of learning otherwise, how irresistibly
she and her garden surface in the mind:
Rosi, among her rosa mundi,
first rose of the world. ⁄⁄

West-Eastern Divan

That Barenboim concert, who knew
it was what we had longed for?
Azar said she learned how to applaud
simply by being there.

Greatness, don't you just love it? I never got over
the smooth wood of Goethe's doorpost.
Weimar always asks us to be noble, suggests
how many conversations there are to be had.

Cold stone hands of the splendid
extend into seating,
facing up; facing down; facing one another
heavily, squarely; learning to talk.

All angles, mind. So bloody uncomfortable,
being upright. Awkward, against inclination -
like taking up a violin
your enemy has just put down.

Like playing, seriously. Like moving through
a forest of staves, without fear. It's not
that languages can't do it; only music
can get there faster - where we long to be.

These little distances,
they're limitlessly disturbing:

Weimar to Buchenwald.
West to East Jerusalem. ⁄⁄

Leavings

They never went back, but it was always
the west, the tug of it
hills waters playboys
hungry and spacious green

The way the grass leans away from the sea

There pronouncing unredeemed
the irredeemable pronoun,
there learning lack,
the lay of the last bachelor

Stories graded like pebbles, ever smaller

Moved further and further toward
town-lights, embraced
the unsuitable friend
(that knowing alternative)

Lost, pure chosen darkness, salt
lying on lips, sighs
in perpetuity, struggles
of legends to be made

The way the grass leans away from the sea //

In the last days

In the last days before it mattered
my sister lived in Kafr Abdou

racketed about the city
in trams, in taxis, on
her bare-headed feet.

Not so long ago
she wrote from the desert, *Everything
is made of salt.*

Out towards Aboukir
cut-throat children giggle and wait.

Message from the dissolving places:
En garde. Don't let
the libraries burn. ⁄⁄

Plaques

If Coker on the whole prefers the brass-plaqued pirate,
Dampier, who went about, swashbuckled, did stuff, bagged
more than one Spanish galleon, *tace et fac**, indeed,

there's nonetheless observance of that other,
the wordy one, who in the better weather
brings in persistent pilgrims, slightly strange.

When the time came, getting him ready,
Churchwarden's work, amounted to locating
his unassuming dust, and a small dead bat.

Then on as quiet a Sunday as you could wish,
his wife was brought to join him, ash with ash:
half funeral, half marriage.
                        And now
it's afterwards, the relatives have left, and all
the grandish folk have scampered back to town,
leaving, complete, the blessing on the wall:

> **&   ESME VALERIE ELIOT**
> **HIS LOVING AND BELOVED WIFE**
> **'in my end is my beginning'**

Quiet there. Close up the door. It's done. ⁄⁄

*The Eliot family motto, loosely translated "Deeds, not words"

Now and again

Your going is like an ebb of the tide,
its waters spreading ripples of your presence
now, and again, about the house.
And fruitless as it would be
to mourn a current,
we know we may not grieve
at so natural an occurrence,
only continue on, in the usual way,
skirting the bobbing water,
the little eddies your going leaves
on the usual strand.
                    You will come back
again, and again, and move among us
with all your old ease, and now
with an added panache,
earned out there, in the wide world,
making waves.
                    Caught in your wake,
touched by small soft reminders
- bath-towel, tea-cup, book -
just now and again we are laved
by a backwash of longing
that makes us catch our breath,
blink salty eyes. ⁄⁄

Stones

The jewels are gone, the box contains only stones,
and try as we might we cannot string them together.
Misshapen, they pile on each other, ungainly weight,
bulk, a foxing heaviness when the lid is down
and the brass bolts drawn across.

What shall be done? The jewels have gone,
the sharp bright shapes with their faery gleam
have melted away under cover of cloud,
are dispersed now, splintered in fragments,
tossed in deep seas, or subsumed into the grandeur
of different crowns. When next we lift the lid
on the dingy ballast left to us
we must not try to ape the ceremonies;
must begin to learn, what others have always known:
how to get by, how to make do with stones. ⁄⁄

On Coker Ridge
("And another thing: you really ought to carry a notebook.")

Tonight the light from the Ridge almost overrides them,
the cross-grained editors, muddy puddles straddling the
                                          byeway, scrawls
of bramble intent on narrowing the passage: tonight
the light
from the Ridge is its own creation,
as of helpless grace, slanting tree-shapes across small
                                          fields and trailing
all summer's wreckage in a melting green glimmer.

Sometimes, this is what it is like, after the storm,
the hills washed of rules, the caviling thoroughfares hidden
in leaf-fall,
the long grass rolling drops of rain about like toys,
the new house that is all windows continuing its merry
                                          rise,
and the heifers chasing each other out of the orchard, apple
                                          time.

If only I carried a notebook
I might write
about the light
on the Ridge
tonight. ⁄⁄

Those office days

Some of those days
towards the end of the 'Sixties:

It is high summer, it is London
having a swelter, so that junior clerks
who on the whole do not like their dungeons
beneath the great offices of state
now welcome that slabby coolness,
return to it after a scorching park lunchbreak,
fiddle thankfully with files.

Not long to go. London
has been swinging some time, girls' dresses are tiny,
traffic stalls and simmers, boys keep bursting into song.

The world of full employment
tempts and beckons.
Behind august marble, someone
is writing *Review in three months*
on stacks and stacks of paperwork,
aiming it at the out-tray
with a fancy flick of the wrist
and an airy, starry smile. ⁄⁄

Grass-green slide

I keep thinking about those river-days,
days of the grass-green slide

Tow-rope behind the punt,
moorings up beyond the backwater,
and that alarming incident
on St Patrick's Stream

Of the deserted house on the eyot,
table laid for elaborate tea,
lace cloth, pink-gilt china,
iced cake, glints of silver

Of how the fact that none of us
could exactly swim, did nothing
to keep us from the fishy sleek
and reedy waters of the inland green

I keep recalling imps of paradise -
mud silting silkily between our toes ⁄⁄

Swan

Weekend water floats it into being,
the Saturday swan,
cold as March along the reaches,
ruffling the surface like wind, its nest
tantalising the towpath.

I dare not.

But I have known swans on the freshet,
swans eirenical, skirting
early bathers, sharing
that especial green:
essays in reflection only.
                    Saturdays
out of school and cycling the riverside,
hanging round the lock with crusts and a swing
on the shifting gate,
                    Saturdays
balancing across the weir
in a gnat-haze:

Days wide as rivers, soft and flecked
with water like cushions in a punt,

days of silted inlets, marsh
marigolds in the backwater,

days altogether moorhenned, splashing
through loosestrife strands towards
so much of summer,

and the Thames
rippling, lapping, for ever floating
the Saturday swan. ⁄⁄

Day Break

Up the stone steps to a froth of blue-
bells ringing with thrush-song, going
out across daisied grass, under the apple-
blossom, along the disappearing
path, beyond the cold and beautiful
stare of antiquity, ducking
under the old arch with its budding
tangle of tendrils, through the new
wet-land willows laid in dancing
rows, past the small eminence
with its wistful god,

Over the new-laid hedge and into
the remnant orchard, stumbling
on moled hillocks, climbing
past a burst of hedge-violets, disturbing
a sudden spray of chaffinch-cry, making
way among heifers and the pearling
early mist rising and rising

The local landscape is part of the ecstasy

And so on
ankle-deep
into another day. ⁄⁄

In the Fishery of Souls

In the fishery of souls
tide-stretched, tide-stranded,
we shoal down time
poor creatures of the drift

now in swift currents helplessly racing
now among pooling shallows lingering

In the fishery of souls
we swim for ever haunted
through ocean's long green
towards the far glimpse

of loveliness unremembered,
towards the one
the perfect
landfall ⁄⁄

The trouble with wolves is

I can no longer look them in the eye. All that
hard-won sang-froid, cultivated courage
undone in a baring of fangs. Abundant,

abandoned, shining among grass-dewed
apples under the Fruit Moon, lie those
who have forgotten how to lack,

while all about them the slinking harsh-jawed
creatures with famished eyes prepare
for a wintry harvest ⁄⁄

The Ermine's Dream

The ermine's dream: a snowfield lit by moonlight
wide and white,
shadows small as the flick of a tail,
a hunting-ground, arena, and delight.

Winding through silence, one cold bite
snaps tight
exactly over the neck of the prey,
closes its moment, inevitable, right.

And returning to stoat-time, back
in the heat
in muddy summer, in the clotted
odour of the rut

that dream, quiet, untold,
lonely and bright,
will stream untouched
beyond the foetid night. ⁄⁄

Night Light

Third night of frost. The hunter's moon
straddles the valley like an overlord
who means seigneurial business.
The field's laid bare, each rimy blade of it
for footsteps to blacken and spoil; each tree
flickers with ashy light along the bough.
The copse lies secretive, a gelid cradle.

Late, late: the star that appeared and hung
under the moon like a harlequin's tear-drop
has sunk down into the land behind the hill.
Then lively, instant, I think of the jovial
wordless boy, who grew up sombre, and now
is lost to all beauty, vanished from the earth
which lies about me, infinitely cold. ⁄⁄

That July in Rome

That July in Rome
when the cistern jammed and we taxied across town
to airy rooms behind the Vatican

Dined at the back of Termini
on a scrub of pavement, *pesce del giorno*,
turned out turbot

Sloped the backstreets
on lazy baking afternoons, our excuse
to linger at Giolitti's

Blinked in Maria Maggiore,
making out the suspicious eyes of saints
taking our modern measure

That July in Rome,
on shining Thursday seeing flags come down
over the Capitol

Waiting to discover
the whole city's glitter hovering suddenly
at half mast

And stopping by some *tabac:*
*"You are from London? - We are so sorry! - But
you have not heard? -"*

That July in Rome
seeking news, making our calls, taking a little comfort
aboard the night bus:

*"Gli operatori
di trasporto di Roma esprimere solidarietà
con il popolo di Londra"*

That July in Rome,
wakeful in darkness suddenly far from home
imagining the dead ⁄⁄

Tall Tale

When the witch was young, and the horse already old
when scars formed in shape that were not yet wounds
when the hill was smoothly devoid of meaning

Meaning
in the day break

there was marked a random band, awkward,
dressed in this and that and tell-tale
tatters of velvet, fanciful,
tights, breeches, wigs: beside the sea
past the crude fisher huts
wickedly parading (and there flapped
vagrant in sea-breeze
skeletons of coloured light),
scrambling nimbly over shingle,
unaccompanied by drum or pipe,

but going with a flourish, going
up the first slope, beyond the church, singing
into that sullen envelope of green, skirts swirling,
heels shining and clicking and knocking and mocking
the abandoned scentless barren tide, calling
to one another in tongues already adjusting
to elsewhere, going reckless, racing
through snickets, high-kicking,
laughing, disappearing
into their own tall tale.

*

Stones attest.
The unkempt pilgrims saunter,
sift the soft past like dust,
for merriment.

Now banners are hung
and tables set *al fresco.*
The story-teller pauses
takes our measure

Nothing will be said
of things once spoiled:

a lifetime's catch
a motley past
nor, witched against her will,
a running girl. ⧫

Irregular Landscape

Irregular landscape:
the thick air of the past
rolls in like old-style fog, or smog,
a thing of story, half-believed:

You couldn't see your hand
in front of your face!
Or the lights of a ten-tonner
until it had run you down.

And in that dangerous time
night-walking in London,
moonlighting from schoolgirl life

I slipped through town on the run
from one Religious, Royal
and Ancient Foundation

wearing soft moccasins
and my first pair of jeans,
padding through South Ken

to keys thrown from high windows,
to lovesongs crooned
in smoky basements,

to breakfast with the bad boys,
back of Harrods,
in the shivering morning. //

All Those Princesses

They always have to be imperiled: by dragons,
naturally, all scales and fangs, although sometimes
it may be only durance vile. Or thrall. Mewed up
in uninspiring turrets, they tend to sew, and wait
until the day of their doom is irresistible.

Then there appears the unlikely rescuer:
a lumpen farm boy, or woodcutter's son,
often a sort of half-wit, aided by luck
and a random dose of magic: good-hearted, yes,
but not expected to go far,
a bit of an accident. And accidentally
he does the slaying, or what it takes, to scale
the turret's heights, and claim his prize.

All those princesses,
putting down their embroideries, extending
blue-veined, flawless, etiolated hands,
gift to the hobbledehoy, perhaps just grateful
that this time he is not, in fact, a toad.
                                  I used to wish,
I still could wish, for just one with a spark
of life about her, who, in taking stock,
chooses, and opts for something different:
who, leaving Dummkopf at the chapel altar,
borrows breeches from the stable-boy,

and saddles up, and makes it through
the castle gate before the grim portcullis
drops down on life; who, unafraid
rides out through ravaged countryside
to build herself a life. She'd tell her story,
repeat it to her children, round the fire
on winter evenings. And wouldn't that
be something like a fairytale? //

Sloping

This summer evening is sufficient shelter: look no further
than small fields swooping past sun-rusted hawthorn,
dog-daisies drifting white towards the dusk. Beneath
those flowering hedges troop, by ancient pathways,
our old confederates, the badgers, trespassers
upon new-fangled fencing, regular as the sun
that sinks now behind the hill behind the hill,
as phantom smoke from the fallen cottage
aimlessly drifts. Once dark, it is no longer
a known and charted space, but slopes
back to its occupants, the carapaced,
or furred, or sliding legless, smooth
within that other dark, the teem
of the deep earth; or lends
itself to country mirth:
all that lost
dancing.

Our feet move very gently, as though to learn
something occult but most necessary, here
among the many different sorts of quiet.
Old coppiced trees have out-stared
all comers. The breath of the grass
would barely disturb a dormouse.
Lie down, lie close: the grace
of this June night will keep
us safe till moon-set,
from every fretful
hunting
wing. //

Acting it out

Theirs is a shadow play, dark dancing,
his, a concrete thing, all grit and gravel.
Too proud to bend, he struts
his angry truth. His syllables
stick their elbows out,
find their own room.

He is the seven-league-booter,
but also the one who knows when
to open up a tear-duct. How
are we in his hands? Capricious,
ogreish, he swallows us,
rolls us round his tongue.

When all the screens are blank
he waves from a tall building
in Geneva, in London,
in Kuala Lumpur, in Dublin.
His light can be seen
disappearing into the last of the dark.

Leave him in the hall of his making,
that great sepulchre of despair.
The crimson chairs are taken away,
the boy is dead, the girl ruined.
What remains to be done? Let us know
no more about him than we can justly bear. ⫽

In Babel we like to think of the Sea

In Babel, we find ourselves thinking of the sea,
our unbuilt boundless boundary:
we imagine the cool wordless lift of it,
the white-flecked fall. We see our past
moving on it, the tiny fleeing figures
in fragile silvered craft, bobbing bereft.

Here in Babel we like to think of the sea,
the curling unsyllabled power of it:
Waves uncircumscribed, waves
swooping and bowing,
waves stretching one upon another
until the horizon is just a rumour.

In Babel we build with wrought phrases, and see
no end to expression: we now have so many
words that could mean The Sea.
Immersed, we continue our upward way:
language flicks at us as fish in shallow pools
flick against the net's dead claw.

Babel is only part of a destiny:
In the dry striving, at our secret hearts,
we conjure an endless grace of ocean;
and in the morning hubbub, wish our very selves
to a place where ancient waters cradle us
in a vast and tongueless roar. ⁊

Ice

Light of pitiless day. In the numb stillness
timbers lie sealed as pent tears
and deep as a drowning
ice catapults into always.
The hapless craft
grazes in frozen fields.

A beauty too cold. Eyes dazzled,
black bread in hand, the mariner
champs on memory
mumbling names
that are now no more
than a matter of faith.

Dreams of small clouds coming and going;
a little tide; sunset; a lifting sail. ⁄⁄

Coker Sonnet

Each look is new, and every look reminds me.
I hardly know these hills, but they collide
with memory, and with the tale that finds me
East Cokering again, to pause outside
the grace-and-favour house, and hear the call
that cobbled up great-grandpa's horrid God
whose hungry habitation needed all
the family, and trickled through the blood
until my father ousted him. Beside
that quiet place, another sweeping track
hoists itself up, and generations ride
their bicycles away. Returning, I look back
at my good fortune. See the hills remain
rolling on westward, in the blissed-out rain. ⁄⁄

Adventry

With beak new-formed, a bird is calling
out of the clement darkness, now
as smoke rises from small valleys
and certain journeys come to an end,
halting tonight in ordinary rooms
where with the evening yellow lamps
begin to shine as usual, visible
through windows unshaded
against the dusk.
Outside
the treading of roads is briefly recorded
by practical purposed boots that must mark the miles
whether through mud or over golden pavements.

Stacked in the hallways, evidence of voyage,
paraphernalia of luck or endeavour,
the trunks and suitcases, the battered canvas
of bags that hold experiments in booty:
enamelled fishes, attar of roses,
cobalt feathers, crimson embroideries,
stolen manuscripts, wrought silver,
bones, a piece of stone worn smooth:
something to marvel at.
    And marvellous
is the tolling note of birdsong,
wild, assured, unknowable,
lifting like an anthem over
oblong panes of light, where none
can tell which travellers' tales
will be believed, which homecoming
will bear the the truth of morning,
nor what strong urge may yet take hold,
turn the weeping eye to stone,
shoe the tired foot with steel.
    It sings,

the helpless bird, that cannot pause
one moment in its commentary,
an unsyllabled, enormous song, which closes
over the edge of these small happenings:
boundless its voice as the vast darkness,
boundless, fluid with distance, elsewhere, beyond. ⁄⁄

Famous

It's a name we knew, when names were something,
when making them seemed hard. What, still alive?
He was old when we were wonderfully young.

Ancient as may be: his small face
shrunk to a white wafer, he watches
quick and wary as a robin.

True survivor from an undignified era,
a sly subversive, naughty-eyed,
his skin so withered up he seems
barely held together. Remember,
while he lived, worlds changed and ended,
and death was his companion;
he spoke his turn, and wrote,
pretended, many things,
saw some of them real.
Ah, famous. We wait on his words.

Then suddenly, we lose him. His gaze
slides past us to a woman,
black-haired, grey-eyed, what he
would call a Beauty. Doing nothing
but stand on her square
foot of carpet, smiling.
And *Ah,* he says, and *Oh,* he says,
and she smiles; and there's our oracle,
old fool like any other,
frail as the dust, breathy, alight, alive. //

News Item 4

Their slot is between the Lottery prize
and Britain's first Gold at the Games.
We are warned of distress. And certainly
they all are dying, though when this film was shot
some of them did not know it.
    This one, for instance,
approaching the camera now, a teen-age boy,
anatomy-lesson limbs, each bone
classically outlined, he shares
a handful of a food we cannot name
with a smaller child, also anonymous.

That proffered hand of his,
that human gesture, kindly, graceful,
might riddle us with shame
if we were not past shaming,

if we were not so far adrift
on wastes of plenty, floating
in the detritus of our difference,
lost between the Lottery prize
and Britain's first Gold at the Games. ⁂

The Conquerors' Catechism

If he had said, the leader who brought us here,
that the first chance is the only chance, maybe
we'd have taken it differently.

If she'd explained, the woman with pearls in her hair,
that the first kiss is the only kiss, maybe
we'd have given it differently.

If they'd spelled out, the scholars we passed on the stair,
that the first word is the only word, maybe
we'd have spoken it differently.

If they had shouted, the firemen jumping clear,
that the first blaze is the only blaze, maybe
we'd have set it differently.

If they'd suggested, the soldiers up for a dare,
that the first blow is the only blow, maybe
we'd have struck it differently.

We took the city, of course, in the final year.
But what is it worth, if we cannot love the land?
What is the thing we do not understand? ◢

A Limestone Woman

Cool as a cave and quiet, she
gleams in the darkness. There
in her unassuming persistence
lies the carving of channels
and the fashioning of stone.
        For her
caverns will come into being
that must occasion wonder,
                    and waterfalls slip
through a maze of gullies
to join the perpetual stream
deep underground.

This is the quality
which will proclaim her
when the picnicking is over:
a natural wonder
of steady endurance, supporting
outcrop and piling stone,
cliffs, and all the motley climbers
out on the towering hills. ⧬

Acknowledgements

Poems previously published in *Acumen, Faith and Hope Anthology, The London Magazine, The New European, Orbis, The Ropewalker, South Poetry Magazine, Timpul, Unearthed.*

Lunch on a green ledge and Down West have been set for solo voice by Andrew M. Wilson. *Beached and Ice* have been incorporated into art works by Ben Gough.

Other anthologies and collections available from Stairwell Books

For further information please contact rose@stairwellbooks.com

www.stairwellbooks.co.uk
@stairwellbooks

Milton Keynes UK
Ingram Content Group UK Ltd.
UKHW010609270923
429428UK00001B/4